Marsha,
You are a SHERO to
many, including me.
Thank you for your
encouragement
and Love.

♡

Venus Jones

10-11-18

Praise for Venus Jones and *She Rose*:

"You are on a ship rocketing to Mars.... It is a joy to experience your work."
— **Nikki Giovanni**, Grammy-nominated Poet and Activist

"I've been involved with the writing community for almost 40 years and Venus has arrived on the scene with as much energy and ability as I have ever seen. I am extraordinarily impressed with her talent...."
— **Peter Meinke**, Creative Writing Chair, Old Dominion University

"...Like hot chocolate on a Midwestern January early afternoon... warm, confident, comforting, and energetic."
— **Floyd Boykin Jr.**, Poet/CEO of *SpokenVizions* Magazine

"It was my honor to share the stage with Venus, she's the real deal."
— **Bob Devin Jones**, Artistic Director, The Studio 620

"...A gardener of the mind. A poet with a green thumb, planting potted images of flowers, rising moons, shining stars and a setting sun."
— **Clarissa Bolding**, Poet and Author of *Life is a Song Worth Singing*

"On a scale of one to ten, a ten is the highest and I give Venus Jones a ten!"
— **Stazja McFadyen**, Poet/Publisher

"Your poetry is thought provoking, original and inspiring. We should all make out as good on our journey as you have so far."
— **Lucinda Clark**, PRA Publishing

"Venus is an insightful poet and a captivating live performer. Since seeing her perform live, I have been recommending her to numerous arts events."
— **Paul Wilborn**, Creative Industries Manager,
      Department of Arts and Cultural Affairs,
      City of Tampa, Florida

"You touched them, you made them reflect, and you entertained them all at once. That's extraoridinary..."
— **Joe DeLuca**, *St. Petersburg Times*

She Rose

on a journey from girl to goddess

Poems of Venus Jones
Edited by Clarissa Bolding

Also by Venus Jones:

Venus to Earth (A trip around the word)
Polly-Ticks
Kwanzaa: 7 Days, 7 Principles
(poems and affirmations for everyday living

The following poems have been printed or recorded elsewhere:

"Amen" and "Poetic Soldier" appeared in *Communication Line*, 2006.
"Heavy" appeared in a Community Action Stops Abuse (CASA) program/brochure,
2005. "Poetic Soldier" performed at the Austin International Poetry Slam, 2004.
"Dali's Daddy Longlegs of the Evening Hope" performed at the Salvador Dali
Museum, 2004. "Poem no. 10803" was performed for Delta Sigma Theta's First
Annual Literary Luncheon, 2003. "I Need a Man" appeared on the Underground
Poetz compilation, 2003. "Gratitude" performed at the Bay Area Spoken Word
Contest, 2002. "Dixie Land" appeared in the *St. Petersburg Times*, 2002.

Please contact:
Venusian Publishing
info@venusjones.com

Fourth Edition
August 2015

Edited by Clarissa Bolding
Book design by Venus Jones
Cover design by Matthew Clark
Cover photograph by Brandall Branch

Foreword

"The Essence of the Muse of Poetry"

For a while, it seemed poetry had lost its way, in the modern world. Only in shadowy coffee houses and out of the way retreats could one bask in the unvarnished fabric of pure poetry. What is pure poetry? It is word-spirit. By that, I mean it is a manifestation of spiritual source set down on paper, and — if one is lucky — recited and received by ear to heart and finally back to the soul, itself. Most Americans never get to experience such a thing because — by and large — we are too busy to stop and listen. For, you see, the appreciation of poetry takes time. It takes a supine attitude that is willing to shut down and shut out those things, which drive people to make hasty decisions. I assure you, poetry is powerful, but never hasty.

Venus Jones is a poet. One cannot say she is a good poet because poetry in and of itself is good. Else it is not poetry. However, we may conscionably agree Venus is a dedicated poet... a poet whose commitment is deep enough that she lives what she loves. Her words in this book are testament to that. So, when you read "She-rose," you, too, will rise to the challenge Venus presents... which is to see her through her poetry... to understand and actually feel her spirit-essence through the wave-length of her metaphor.

And did you know? Venus Jones — whose name is taken from Venus De Milo, maybe? — is every bit the poetess she claims to be... because indeed, she claims it! Is she as compelling and as powerful as she will become, one day? Who knows? It is not ours to care. In poetry, only the now is important. So, read "She Rose," now... and be satisfied that you are in the midst of a child of the Muse.

Peace and Poetry,

James E. Tokley, Sr.
Poet Laureate
City of Tampa

In memory of Rose Mary Long, 1953 - 2003

Your faith was evident every day
Every day you had to chase that dirty sugar away
But it never made you sour
Not even in your last hour
You were as patient as Mary
You were a resilient Rose
I will never forget the way you wiped my nose
The way you took me in and made me feel as your own
You stuck up for me when I was a child
I miss you now that you're gone
I'll never forget your song
Your time short, your spirit Long

Table of Contents

Acknowledgement

I am grateful for my dream developers and my dream destroyers as they have provided the sunshine and rain for my growth.

You know who you are.

Introduction

"A nation can rise no higher than its women." — *African proverb*

There's a Goddess within all of us. Yet, in my travels, I've observed that many women continue to be oppressed, suppressed, and generally stressed. Women, often seen as either angels or devils, are truly the backbone of society and should be regarded as such.

For centuries, governments, religions, races, and creeds of nearly every culture have considered women to be servants to men and second-class citizens, who work more and are paid less across the globe. When the nurturing God was replaced with the God of war, it also became common practice to remove the word "Goddess" from our speech to demonize the nurturer and all that is natural which eventually led to the exploitation of Mother Earth.

In recent years we've seen a sparked interest in the study of peace, feminine energy, and the power of Goddess language and symbols. I don't feel the need to debate the gender of the supreme deity. I honor Truth, whether it comes from a man or a woman. Yet the "mother" remains as the first teacher and, in this book, it is my desire to lift her up with overdue praise.

> "Even more countries have understood that women's equality is a prerequisite for development."
> — *United Nations Secretary-General and Nobel Peace Prize winner* **Kofi Annan**

There are unsung "sheroes" among us with Goddess-like strength waiting to reclaim their personal power. I want these women and the underrepresented everywhere to rise to their fullest potential so they may promise every nation a brighter and more beautiful future. The goal is equal treatment in the home and in the government, so we may end poverty and sustain development. I've included poems that share stories of when I chose to rise on a particular occasion, and I also offer inspirational metaphors that assist me on my journey.

My book "She Rose" will lead to a companion CD and/or workbook called "Thorns", a stage production, and an overall mission to increase the visibility of diverse voices who are willing to stand up for their rights to be human and humane. This is a book for anyone, male or female, who wants to connect with a Mother and Father God reclaiming all that is divine within.

Why I write

The Creator still speaks and sometimes through me
Finding inspiration in everything I taste, touch, hear, smell, and see
My ego grows weak
When producing a clean slate
I wait for divine direction
The mission is to stay in the seeker section
Seeking to speak the truth

I write to inspire and spread proof
Write to heal
I write to make things tangible and real
Write to recite
I write to receive
Write to every color, age, orientation, and creed
I write in the morning
Write in the middle of the night

Sometimes words turn on the light and get me out of bed
Learned to keep a pad and pen near my head
Your average creative artist is a tortured soul
Some words are dark and some words have attached goals
Some are light, bold, and blue
Some words haunt you
Until you transform their stage
Some words produce rage and are spicy like Rosemary and Sage
It is a contest of ideological compromise
If they told you metaphors always win, they spread lies

I will never write to simply entertain
I write to honor those who came before me and were slain
Those who had to create pen names or be jailed like the insane
I write so my visions will never be chained

The Pledge

I promise to bring renewed hope and courage
to people who's pain and suffering has been felt in my heart

To the Most High, I grant my life because I trust
I was given a unique clarity from the start
I will never stop learning how to receive your blessing
I do not stand for fear of you or any other
For I love you
Like my kindred
Like my father
Like my mother
So teach me how to use this love as an art
I surrender my all to you
So that we may never part

The little girl in me

Untamed and running wild
My inner child
She has a lust for life
It's always Spring in her feet
The sun shines when she smiles
Love this girl who lives for peace
This child who wants so much to be free
This girl who will live and love eternally
Until she can make all creation see
That true freedom is born not in I but in we

for the budding mind

My Story

Played a victim but today, prefer to choose the role of survivor
Reunited with my original lifelines and, like the oak,
I'm growing roots above and under ground
It was Langston's mother who said, "Life ain't no crystal stair"
So I sing in rain like Kelly and dance like Astaire
Knowing Euro spirituals will ascend me higher

Sometimes I paint my face with that upside down frown for your pleasure
Not proud of each picking
But everything on my plate I treasure
Everything on my plate I chew
Slowly savor what's good flavor
When biting down on an unexpected crunch, I spit it out
Yet I've acquired a taste for bittersweet lemons
Peeled back man-made layers to tease
I still scream hallelujah when I shout

Earned my clout, claimed a crown
Don't hide my riches or the dark eye bags, I once wore around town
Tears were so heavy, they pounded semi-permanent puddles on my face
Tears use to fill my room so fast, I thought I'd drown in a salty sea of distaste
Have soundtracks like a lady wailing the blues
Waking up to four in one bed and the smell of yellow pools
Been packed in like sardines in a car from ceiling to floor
Had windows you'd wipe every 20 seconds just to see a bit more
That's me

Been the sophisticated middle class
Been a low down country bumpkin
These facts about my history are no mystery
For those who seek and listen with open hearts, closed eyes
Blessed with many blue skies
Given so much, barely speak of what I lack
Don't want to end up at another crossroad called compromise
Like the last bright sunny day, with hog humidity on the rise

Abandoned at the age of two
Caused one of the walking dead to get so jealous
She attempted to vex me with voodoo
A suspicious package, labled handle with care
The torn or broken despised my qualities
Seemed to be polished and rare

Same loving flock that gave this Spring chicken training and sense of value
Occasionally exposed me to dreary domestic issue
Cried fearing my mother and father would beat each other red,
Wounded with verbal rocks and boulders left indentations in my bean head
But I'm still me
Still the same two year old who would say, "Gimmie some... Gimmie!"
Especially if it's free

Devour library books with delicious words that marinate on your mind
A craving carnivore who loves the taste of Christ's body
One day drank some of his blood
It's a fountain of youth and it seems to taste like wine
Been drunk ever since off the holy and the divine

She Rose (for some of my female heroes)

With the power of her presence and the strength of her fight,
Her words caused wrinkled men to question slavery,
weary women grew imaginary wings for solo flight.
Sojourner rose. Sojourner Truth, she rose.

I know why the caged bird sings.
Oh my, a landmark of firsts on a broken wing.
Although she's raped at seven and a mother at sixteen,
with a past rooted in pain. She said, "I rise," and her poetry sings.
Maya rose. Maya Angelou, she rose.

She stood in muddy water and created clean lines with a clear vision.
Hate drew an incision across her beautiful wall of monumental art.
Like a veteran soldier in a bulldozing battle, rage surfaced but
ancestress women led her to pick up the pieces of her beating heart.
Maya rose. Maya Lin, she rose.

She loved one person at a time, a shining example of the divine
A steady flame and pillow for the restless, unwanted, unloved, and poor,
Fed haunting hunger with her hands and opened up the stickiest door.
Theresa rose. Mother Theresa, she rose.

She was a union spy with eyes in the back of her head.
Over a thousand crept in her footsteps or followed where she led.
She forced them with a gun and said, "Live free or die!"
This female Moses taught them to walk, run, or fly.
Harriet rose. Harriet Tubman, she rose.

She was called mentally ill and worse, a traitor and a liar.
She was grilled in judiciary fire.
Levitating above sex books, videotapes, and lies,
she helped remove muffles on silent cries.
Anita rose. Anita Hill, she rose.

She said, "Feel what you can not touch."
She laughed at the thought of living with a crippling crutch.
When they said, "You're blind, deaf, and disabled!",
she couldn't understand their limited view.
She saw, heard and spoke like a spiritual guru.
Helen rose. Helen Keller, she rose.

9

At fifteen she fought back against Little Rock, big fireballs, and acid attacks.
In 1954 angry white mobs were ordered to open up the school door to blacks.
There was no dance or after class play with a bounty on your head.
"Dignity just like freedom is a state of mind," her grandmother said.
Melba rose. Melba Beale, she rose

She's floating on air in a silver space suit with a fearless smile.
She holds three degrees in hand; they seek to clone her mental style.
This rising star brings blueprints to the Peace Corps
and measures the length of courage and mental vigor.
Mae rose. Mae Jemison, she rose.

She sang of rotting bodies in America's very first protest song.
Her life short, and the scar left on her soundtracks lingering and long.
"Strange Fruit" would be read on the Congress floor
because of the love she blew into an open sore.
Billy rose. Billy Holiday, she rose.

She didn't spend time plucking her brows, knowing inner beauty grows.
In a bright big Mexican dress she rebelled with art that tangoed on toes.
Her canvass celebrates a life of broken bones, fruits, and a thick thorn.
She lived a life full of authentic expression in her search to be reborn.
Frida rose. Frida Kahlo, she rose.

A humane example, before she took a stand by keeping her seat.
She chose to fight despite the risk of a thrashed skull or dangling feet.
Rosa rose. Rosa Parks, she rose.

Lena Horne, Bessie Coleman, Angela Davis,
Dolores Huerta, Toni Morrison, Ida B. Wells,
Shirley Chisholm, Oprah Winfrey, Fannie Lou Hamer
Barbara Jordan, Eleanor Roosevelt, Mary McCloud Bethune....

Each one, a rose among thorns, and every vision is in full bloom.
If we were in ancient Kemet, Nefertiti would've granted them tombs.

But the thankless are more than a few.
My mamma Rose, and your mother rose, giving birth to something new.
They rose like blossoming babies, budding freshly formed leaves,
quenching the taste of light morning dew.

I need all of them to remind me, that there is a shero in me
and there is a shero in you.

Gender Rules (for the rule breakers)

Girls' rule

The girl was told by her big sister
to be sweet and tender.
"Don't look like Flappa Fanny,
but be sure to wear high heels on your feet.
With some pretty pink wrapping
and a name brand label,
you might even resemble Grade A meat."

Now the girl had something to prove
to her mother who said,
"Girls don't anger, fuss, or fight."
To the young man who said,
"Her hair just doesn't look right."
Her womanly mission
was to be the symbol of beauty
and serve him with good cheer.
If the girl didn't measure up,
she'd learn to say, *"I'm sorry, dear."*
"Look at me! I can do splits,
the flip, and that pretty twirl."
He'd say, *"Don't forget to smile,*
show more teeth. That's good. Good girl!"

She learns that good girls only speak when spoken to.
They stay in the shallow end,
away from those who question and seek.
A good girl doesn't worry her pretty little head.
She just relaxes and wonders, *"Do I look a little too well fed?"*
So she puts more paint on her face. She puts on satin and lace.
She lives in fear that one day he will be displeased with her tacky taste.
"What about a little tuck here?
A diamond in my ear or implants might look fine."
She's a manufactured baby doll,
and her future's riding
on his assembly line.

Boys' Rule

The boy was told by his big brother *to "play with a heavy hand.*
Keep the pressure high, stay on top of the game, or
dive into the agony of defeat."
With his wit he could turn a girl into a trick, if she lived to give the treat.
So he worked hard to buy some fancy bait, the hooks and the shiny tools.
No one taught a course on how to be a good boy in his grammar schools.
The boy has a conquest that his mannish friends believe he cannot lose.
This is why you won't find the controls of his vehicle set on cruise.

This is for his father who said,
"He isn't hard and slick enough."
This is for his mother who said,
"He needs to be rich, sexy, and buff!"
His manly mission was to protect and provide, until his dying day.
Those little boys who aren't up for the task and have little cash tend to say,
"What about the man?
Who's going to protect the man?"
When there is silence, some of the weak go astray.
Others simply pray to the Super Man above,
while the rest realize they're gay.

He must be the strongest in the sport.
He must be the fastest on the court.
This boy has a conquest he cannot lose.
You can find him playing the role of the accused.
His love will hit you like a rock
His only concern his family jewels
When abiding by these gender rules

"What is most beautiful in virile men is something feminine; what is
most beautiful in feminine women is something masculine." —
Susan Sontag

12

My friend

There's a puddle on the pavement
that ripples with the wandering wind.
The thunder in the distant echoes.
A warning of what's to come again.
Only five feeling mighty
in a small world. Afterall,
I had my baby blue goulashes.
It was all about my splash. Not the fall.

I was big enough to find a friend.
Who loved to skip to my beat.
She knew how to hopscotch.
How to share her rice treat.
Mrs. Lewis fears the storm. She points to
dark grey clouds overhead. She begs
us to return inside. We want to fly
higher on swings instead.
We're spinning on the merry-go-round.
It all blends together that way.
We create our own signature swirl.
We could sniff for rain forever. We stay.

But the wind almost knocks her down.
A gust circles around my new freind.
She tries to run faster. Teacher scolds.
Deaf we pretend. Laughing at my dizzy spell
and the force of a zephyr. So free.
Just about to jump off and she says,
"Wait, push me!"

"True friendship is like a rose:
we don't realize its beauty until it fades."
— Evelyn Loeb

13

Daisy *(for a flower child)*

My garden is like a choir full of red roses.
Pink azaleas sway in the breeze.
We placed dazzling daffodils in the back row.

One iris — ever so blue — sings in the center.

My orchids are a praise team in full dress.
Only two stems resemble berries before bloom.

But it's a troublesome weed that delights her.
It was her sunshine, now it's her fuzz ball bliss.

She jumps on long blades of green grass in the backyard.
Leaping at the sight of a dirty hairy disc.

The sight of dandelions makes Daisy forget her name.
I call her to the dinner table. She can't hear me.

She's too busy prancing like Ms. Buttercup.
She's blowing white feathers into the wind.

She and her neighborly pigtailed friend,
make wishes, they giggle and grin

and time stands still.

Here's to Mother (for Rosa Mae)

She's a pistol, and the queen of Southern backwoods slang
Rosa Mae is the name
She likes to point with her index finger when she scolds
"You gone catch, the Tee bees! I told you to come in from the cold."
She'll warm you up with oatmeal and hot cream of wheat
On a gray and windy day.
"Do you have on your long johns Tori, Dee Dee, Rosemary, I mean, Faye?"
She has six children and 21 grandchildren. 30 great and one great-great
So when she does a roll call, you'll hear your name... just a little late

She'll use the green broom to sweep up kitchen dust balls and hair
She loves to sing, *Lord, I need thee,* with a slow and traditional flair
At night it was, "Sleep tight, and don't let the bed bugs bite."
In the morning it was,
"Hurry up, stand up straight, and tuck your shirt in right!"
"Girl, I think you still smell musty, and boy, comb your nappy head."
Never looked like Tabby Habby, we learned to value presentation instead
Yes, she was harsh but we were respectful and clean
Everywhere we went, we looked like a black Brady Bunch team

Before we ate breakfast, lunch, or dinner she'd always bless the food
If you started eating too fast, she'd give you that look that screams,
"Don't be rude!"
At 770 Carlysle Street, it's customary
To give thanks for what is given, that's the rule
If we slipped up and forgot, we started looking like that full moon fool
Even at 85, no one really wants to get on her bad side
Do you have some really thick skin or good place to run and hide?
You say payback is a Mother
That could be why every one loves to call her that name
She don't take no mess, Lord have mercy
I declare, she's a hot flickering flame

You don't need a "down payment on a mosquito jacket,"
To be tested or approved
Just know her weakness:
Cash money and some fancy high-heeled shoes

On Sunday morning, there wasn't a discussion or plan
We just knew to be dressed
"What's done in the dark will come to the light,"
So we had to repent and confess
Didn't want to make that list
She believed some kids belonged "up under the jail."
It's usually a mannish filthy mouth or
the one who looks like Flappa Fanny or Jezebel

Had to switch up or return a few skinny branches
From the tree, three or four times
She never spared the rod; I wasn't a spoiled child
She whipped my sassy wanna-be back-talking behind
If anyone gets hurt or runs into a case of the stomach flu
She'll say, "Here's what you do, eat a spoonful of this Vicks.
"You have to feed a cold and starve a fever, and I got all the tricks."

She raised me to be thrifty
Something was made out of nothing
She had a rich look
She knows what scripture you need to memorize
It's Psalms 23 in The Good Book
Only God knows where I'd be
If it wasn't for her militant way and passionate prayer
I'm so glad she put a sense of pride in my mane
And let me roar in her lair

*"Some are kissing mothers and some are scolding mothers,
but it is love just the same." — Pearl Buck*

Beauty of a mother (for Mommy)

The beauty of a mother is seen
when she naturally wipes her little girl's nose.

The beauty of a mother is seen
when she tickles her little boy's toes.

A glimpse of beauty is found in the way she brushes her baby's hair.
The way she gives you that stern look that screams, "Don't go there!"
The beauty of a mother is demonstrated in a man who treats women right.

The beauty of a mother is seen in a woman,
who doesn't claw her way towards catfights.
You can find more beauty in her taste in books than her fancy looks.

Her beauty can also be tasted in a homemade pound cake, make no mistake.
Beauty is seen in her loving eyes that welcome you even when you're late.
The beauty of a mother is seen pushing a stroller in aisle five.
The beauty of a mother is loud when the concert is live.

She's in the center of the crowd in the front row, shouting, "Go'on ahead!
That's my baby! Will you look at her go!"

She coaches and provides with very little rest.
Guess Mamasita really does know beauty best.

"A mother is not a person to lean on but a person to make leaning unnecessary." — Dorothy C. Fisher

Good Hair

She said, "God don't like ugly!"
I thought does that mean God don't like me?
Because God must have been joking when my hair was made nappy.

Wait! Someone said, God don't make mistakes.
God seems to think diversity is great!
Yet, my culture is still in a process debate
because straight is considered good.
Kinky curls are bad and bring self-hate.
So I long for hair that stretches long.

Sometimes I want sun kissed locks and even eyes of light sea blue.
When God made my eyes rich with melanin,
mysterious, deep and dark as his midnight sky too.
But I'm still healing from what I'd been told
in those advertising messages
that often make my natural beauty feel cold.
I've learned to embrace the coolness of my natural shade knowing
God loves the coarseness of my grade.
I noticed my natural crown is shaped similar to the trees...
I wear it when I no longer feel the need to please
those who stare with that confused glare,

Asking,
"Are you mixed, you have good hair?"
But my grandma would say,
"It use to be good, now it looks like mooda grass!"
I'd say...
"Don't you think that's what makes it last?"

My hair is resistant.
My hair is strong.
My hair is right and can never be wrong.
It can take braids, chemicals, waves, and weaves.
That's a lot for the bored and political naïve.
One day I may flip on, sew on or press on for fashion sake,
That'll be a day when I'm feeling free to relate.
How free?
As free as a natural blonde in a dashiki and plaits...
Truth is I'm still having good hair and bad hair debates.
But my hair is all good, even in its most nappiest state.

Talking Back

Didn't expect the sting to linger so long.
Think I felt my brain shake as my eyes did a final roll back.
Before I could blink I was put down with a smack.
Felt the imprint at the base of my neck.
The swinging hoop fell from my earlobe and I held my breath.

Standing in a cold frostbitten glare.
Instantly saddened with shivering shame.
Instantly centered in fear and pain.
The sting traveled from my face into my heart.
Wanted to crawl up in the corner and die.
Like a spider in the fetal position I wanted to draw in my limbs.
When that single tear escaped from my right eye.

It ran down the center of my cheek.
It landed on top of my throat.
Wiped the long line clean with the back of my hand.
And a pool of boiling words simmered down in my gut.
Went from hot to cool but I lost my strut.

I was strong,
        now I'm meek.
I was speaking,
        now I'm weak.

"No, I am not grown.
No, I am not yet on my own.
I will watch my tone."

I learned to lower the bass in my tone.

Spare the rod and spoil the child.
Turn spice into something mild.
Make that cookie break and crumble.
Make that spirit humble.
So now you can hear me mumble.
Almost knocked out the light that made me shine.
This training punctured my soul and saved my behind.
And if there's a thin line between love and hate
There's a double-edged sword in the abuse or excuse debate.

They say, loud mouth children need to be shunned.
And if the slap doesn't stick, use the belt, or mamma's gun.
Master said,

"Beat them into submission.
Next time they'll ask permission.
No longer will they question authority or step on toes."

But if you want a bright idea or a fresh opinion...it's...

Opinion? I don't know if I have one.
Um? Do I have one of those?"

You seek the confident and direct response
of the next Soujourner Truth.
Be patient.
I'm still defrosting the tongue of fire
that was frozen in my youth.

Don't You? (for nobody special)

"You think you somebody!"
Why, yes I do,
The question is, don't you?
Don't you think that you're somebody too?

"You've got some nerve!"
I have nerve, heart, and a clue.

"You think you cute!"
I *am* cute!
I am happy!
I am healthy!
I am confident!
I am successful!
I am grateful!
I'm a child of God, too.
I am whatever I say I am.
This little light of mine,
I'm going to let it shine, through and through.
We are born to manifest God's glory.
I am not going to bury my gifts out of fear.
I do not fear failure.
Nor do I fear displeasing many or a few and please, don't you.
Don't you!

"The most common way people give up their power
is by thinking they don't have any."
— Alice Walker

Gratitude

I am grateful for hope, health, humility, the breeze
The way the Earth rotates on its axis with such ease
For words, so many languages available to explore
For birds singing outside my door
For the crack in the sidewalk and the way babies make me goo-goo talk
I'm grateful for the way you are always in my way on the road
The way a frog differs from a toad
The way you whisper like no one can hear
The way we welcome truth and have not one but two listening ears
The way you spread love,
creating an atmosphere that resembles heaven above
And there's a slight change in weather
The way you reflect light, and you thought I didn't notice
How we laugh at those with little sense, and compare Marvin to Otis
The way good food and good music always takes me back
The way you teach me to concentrate on what I have instead of what I lack
I don't always say it, but sometimes I feel the need to spray it and
I'm grateful for the spit, because it just means you know I'm legit
I am grateful for any feeling that stirs up such passion
I am thankful for your compassion for simply hearing me out
I am grateful for the time and place in which I live
I may not be totally free but I'm no longer terrorized
Like my brown ancestors and many female sisters before me
I am thankful for your friendly smile and land we worked so hard to obtain
That will be ours in a while
The way we laugh and
We seem to dance and prance about in the night
We still dance even when we've lost sight
So I'm thankful that I can take a journey
on the transportation of my choice
Whether it be my mind or your voice
For the special way I see you, hear you, feel you
Love the fact that I can be so real with you
I'm thankful for your scent because I believe you were sent
bearing flowers, thank you for those flowers you may bring to my cold feet

I am grateful for this life my love
Gratitude is so neat

I'd Prefer (for the forgotten names)

No you didn't create this language.
So when you rearrange it I tend to squint and blink.
What does she mean? Is she calling me a bitch or just playing today?
I'd rather you just greet me with, "Hey!"
But not around my mamma because, "Hay is for horses!" she would say.
It's all relative, but we're talking about me and what I like and dislike, ok?
You are still my friend but I really don't aspire to be your gangsta bitch.
And dear brother why do you want to be mistaken for a runaway thug?
Don't you know the hunt is on for a Polaroid shot that looks like your mug?
Thugs are suicidal with no respect to any life there is or ever was.
Now what happened to the twin towers, that's gangsta.
When you plot murder you must be willing to die 'cause
as it says in song, real gangstas don't live that long.
So do you aspire to live or die, for what and why?
Why you wannabe a nigger?
The word is like whiplash.
The whip lands on my neck, the lash is imprinted in the DNA on my back.
Don't have time to turn around and check the skin you're in
just to see if the definition is in tact.
I'm not your nigger if you're white.
I'm not your nigger if you're black.
Some still try to embrace me with,
"What up hoochie..." at *my* door.
Don't aspire to be a pimpette, a hoochie, or professional whore.
Don't care for the image on the mic, in the studio, or on the dance floor.
The image helps some starving artists earn more money
when divide and conquer is the goal.
My choice is to uplift you with these words
Want to keep my valuable soul.
My integrity... not for sale.
Let's produce more heaven on Earth,
God knows we've seen enough hell.
Knowing you get tired of hearing the same ol' song
Knowing you get sick of bumping backaching blues.
So I refuse to get drunk off booze, won't start talking smack about past duels.
Know my worth so I don't have to prove my territory or wave my gun.
Offering you words on a cloth to dry your tears
Want you to dust off so you'll shine like the sun.
Won't see me constantly using sex as a tool to reel in prey.
So get behind me Satan, I found my validation on the inside today.
Prefer to represent more than glorified violence and superficial sex.
Believe we can always evolve to what's next.

23

Why broadcast propaganda for the racist?
It's more ammunition that they can use.
Yet, *I am* whatever I say *I am*,
Really don't care about their views.
But just do me a favor and show some discretion with your tongue?
It is written that every word you speak has energy... every single one.
When you build on a foundation that's based in shame,
your history and your teacher will enter the frame.
The slave master knew the power of language when he changed your name.

I'd prefer

that you embrace me with

"Hi Mamma!" or "There's what I call a sister!"
"The woman...Black Pearl!"

Rather than

"What up my little nigga?"
"My gangsta bitch-dog!", or
"My girl....the hoochie-hoe!"

Let me know you've heard me loud and clear before I go
If you know the nature of the drill then say, "Yes, ma'am."

I need you to respectfully say, "Yes, ma'am."

Because in the spirit of my noble ancestors,

"I told you so!"

*"Most people ignore most poetry,
because most poetry ignores most people."
— Adrian Mitchell*

24

Missing Ankh

The cross and the sword are both shaped the same.
Disconnected lines are a reflection of his circumcised pain.

On a chain that's wrapped around his neck, he bears a cross
It's missing the nurturing loop; the cord has been cut
Here lies a newborn with eyes frozen from too much estrogen loss.
Some flags stay at half-mast in The Divided States
where infants suffer from symptoms of a killer flu.
During the last election debate, stats regarding blacks and HIV were given.
The financial response in 2002 was more shocking than the verbal
which was, "Who knew?"

Little to nothing was done or said
about blue eyed children lying dead in all those bright and dark hallways.
Never really listened to Marvin's song.
Never really cared about what's going on
with brown eyed girls or boys in the hood,
"Anyways! Gangs bring down the grimy ghettos."
A mother with three jobs bangs her head on the wall in search of green relief.
Her gifted son lived with countless threats,
before a cop's bullet gave him peace.

We travel to the Middle West and find
sour milk spilled on a pink prom dress.
Black letters on yellow tape are blowing in the wind,
Like the crusaders we charge in to a schoolyard full of white chalk lines.
Lil' Joe's being tucked under
his last sheet on Plantation Drive for the last time.

Can you imagine
a news team around sixteen year old Keisha's body on MLK?
Can you see the last flash from the camera that confirms it's too late to pray?

What's done in the dark will show up on the shore on his trip to the lake.

Every sixty seconds a woman feels the heavy weight of rape.

Is it a symbol of death or is it a crime that I still want you to see?
If only the strong survive, what happens to me and three million meek?
What happens to the poor and homeless children of the wealthiest's weak?

Some quote the book of Revelations and speak of doomsday.
Soon and very soon we are going to see the King, that's what they say.

But first the meek will inherit what's left of the earth.
If that's so, when will the crooked and the straight piper begin to pay?

The woman with the outstretched arm is slowly sinking into quicksand.
The king of the world isn't hungry but he's biting Mother Nature's hand.
His brother's grumbling belly gives him no sense of gratitude or relief.
The king drops some crumbs so he won't question the cause of his grief.

He grants death before life, seeking judgment more than heaven's grace.
The cross and the sword he wears protects and scars his smirking face.

He drinks the blood that drips and sleeps sound amoungst the lowest in spirit
There are dead men walking
Wearing masks that resemble the risen and resilient.

"Our scientific power has outrun our spiritual power. We have guided missiles and misguided men." — Dr. Martin Luther King Jr.

Blue Book

still searching for the book that she uses
it's a royal blue
paper back book

can't find it
in my night dreams
she said, I'd memorize it
she knew I'd recite it

she stood there wise and full of grace
stared me in the face

she spoke
it was silent and we listened
the breaks
the breaths
the words were as sweet as the scent
of berries riding on Summer breezes
we became light

she was one person
now two
now when she appears
the tan hood she wears covers nearly all her senses
only her eyes and bangs peek through

her eyes glow and syllables flow like rivers
down a levitating stream that directs you to a starlit sky
i sit at her feet and in the open I cry
two heavy tears
as she pours her liquid truth into my ears
I'll be searching for that blue book for years

Cry Out

From now on when I cry
I'll feel no fear as a tear draws near
I'll let it drop down my face
And I will feel no disgrace
I'll know it's strength I'm showing
I'll express all that is bare and true
Since trust is found in eyes that flow freely when they need to
For they are the windows of my soul
From now on this is the deal
I will cry and I will heal
From now on I won't try and stop it
I won't apologize and choke
I won't try and mask it and resort to dope
From now on when I cry I'll hold my head up high
And breathe with ease, naturally releasing the chemicals of despair
From now on when I cry I'll know that I'm humane
And my tears show I really care
It won't matter anymore if they stare
It won't matter anymore if they dare to
call me a little girl, wussy, sissy, and weak
I will know that denial of struggle
Is for those poets who don't speak
but hide their love and hoard their pain out of fear
We know pain shared is pain divided
But some still claim that every message should be delivered on a dry face
Yet I feel no disgrace
                    I cry out
They believe crying is only done in a dark space
Yet I feel no disgrace
                    I cry out
From now on when I cry
I'll cry with a purpose and I'll know why
From now on...I will never hold tears IN the eye
                    I cry out

"In the midst of my crying, I felt my freedom coming."
— Iyanla Vanzant

28

No More

Whenever you are feeling blue or a little down
Just remember I too have worn that frown
It's not just you who feels stuck like glue

I know it's a system
A cycle established in the past
Set up to keep us dosing
But it won't last
When you open your eyes
To any sign of crooked compromise
Those covered lies you despise will rise

It's night and
We have all been led
by those without sight
Please allow me to shed light

There are only three things to do
When it's hurting you

Confront the problem
Ignoring the problem is number two
Number three is leaving
That's what I plan to do
I've already exhausted number one and two
It's a messed up situation when you have a history of
blood, sweat, tears, humiliation, and constant frustration

My anger fueled my determination
when I realized my pain was their inspiration
Love and knowledge of self are keys, that unlock this door
And I shall return
to the stage of victimization
No more

"There came a time when the risk to remain tight in the bud was more painful than the risk it took to blossom." — Anais Nin

I need a man

I can do bad by myself
I don't need nobody else
I work day and night
Night and day to pay the bills of yesterday

It's okay and it's all right
You know I can make wrong right without a fight

Understand I need a complete companion
Someone who's down for the grand haul
I'm talking about that person who will pick me up when I fall
What you want isn't what you say
Your actions speak louder than your words on any given day
But you're going to play me like the fool anyway
When I gave you my love and I gave you my time
But you can't spare a dime
It's not your lack of funds, but your dead spirit
That's what has me on the run
I don't have room for dead weight
Since day one I set it straight

Why don't you come real, come correct?
Is it that you're not ready yet?

If you would've told me upfront
I would've understood
That you were a boy, on the threshold of manhood
Now I must question, if it was all just for show
That's right, I'm getting out this game, but it's a shame
It's a shame I no longer feel the same
Because my baby still calls out your name

I'm a single mother and I'm doing all I can
But I don't need a boy to help me raise a son
I need a man

"Son, always tell the truth. Then you'll never have to remember what you said the last time." — Sam Rayburn

Are you a good man? (for my brother)

Good men look past the color of your eyes and into your heart.
A good man always gives you space but never really wants to part.
A good man may even say your name around his co-workers or crew.
He loves to say, "My wife and I" when he speaks of you.
When you're in an argument that leads to a verbal fuss or fight,
he'll find a way to a middle ground before the end of the night.

I've known gentlemen who lend a hand and know when to open a door.
I've known good men who don't feel the need to compete or score.
A good man picks your ego up off the floor if you fumble or fall.
He'll kiss away the pain and respectfully return every call.

Good men tend to serve their community and make the voiceless speak.
This kind of man, has a spirit so strong, your knees get weak.
The ones who posts love notes that inspire you to dream and fly.
He'll live a life based in principles than just lie down and die.
He's the one, who brings home dinner, just to put a smile on your face.
A good man delivers you plants and roses to perfume your place.
I've known good men who are married but still set lunch and dinner dates.
He even threw out whiskey to help her discover her good traits.

A good man will stand beside his queen on that dark and dreary day.
I've seen them kneel down to give thanks, asking God to lead the way.
A good man reads books on how to maintain family and cash.
A "real" good man has that polite patience, which often resembles class.
I've known good men who plan surprise parties to fill an empty home.

This kind of man will tell you if he feels the urge to roam.
A good man listens with a third ear when you talk.
He even knows the value of a good star lit walk.

I've known good men who love to massage away stress
Greets you with hugs, a candle light, or a bubble bath and says, "Rest."
A good man can smile and make the sun shine during stormy weather.

He's really good if he tends to ask, "How can I do better?"
For all those reluctant men who are still wondering,
"What does *she* have to do?"
All of the above qualifications apply when in search for a good woman, too.

Diamond

You are my diamond

I know it is tough
You are my diamond in the rough

Diamonds are lumps of coal
that stuck to the goal

Their mission is to shine through the darkest day
You've already proven you have the power to stay
That's why I fell in love this way

You are so clear and so rare
I'm often blinded by the glare

Diamond, you became this girl's best friend
the one on which I can depend

and now you want me to lend you my hand,
after you've captured my heart
I do, because I don't ever want to be apart

Now before you shower me with earthly coal or
search the sea for a worthy enough element for me
Know that you are my diamond
Can't you see?

You are my diamond
and that's more than enough for me

You represent forever, infinity, and a day
The love that we share nothing,
Nothing, not even time can take this love away

"I would rather have roses on my table than diamonds on my neck."
— Emma Goldman

True Love (for the L.O.M.L.)

I remember the first time you finished my sentence without a clue?
I never had a want or need because you already came through
One day we were laughing and
I looked in your eyes and found something new
A twinkle as special as morning dew
I noticed the tulips seemed brighter
My heart in public seemed lighter
And It didn't matter our surroundings
It was just us two
My love garden grew

Everything is different now

Something similar to nothing I'd ever knew
My fear was things might change
Then I realized to stay the same was insane
I was grateful but asked God for guidance
When things seemed too good to be true

Later I acknowledged the love felt
When you'd speak my name
The way you asked for my hand
The comfort of your gentle touch
The way you defined man
My heart would beat fast when I'd receive your call

Slowly but surely
No longer questioned the color of love at all
I see canary yellows, grand greens, royal reds, and beautiful blues
A rainbow, a multi-colored hue
A reflection of hope, everyday is brand new
It's you and me
It's me and you
And you'll live forever in my heart
For this is love
For this is true

May Flowers (for a sweet heart)

May I have a flower?
May each petal soothe my curiosity and relieve the strain?
May I stop to smell the red roses and pick petunias in bloom?
May I get pollen on my chin and clovers in my hair before June?
May a bouquet of beauty glide through my fingers like silk?
May I be the baby and this blossom my milk?
May I stroll to find pure sweet delight?
May the crops be ripe?
May the aroma of plump and juicy pears and oranges feel the air?
May I reap the fruit of my care?

Healthy Seeds

Plant healthy seeds and reap what you sow.
If you water the thought it will grow.
Someone said, "You don't count; you're weak and small!"
Are you shining beams on that limiting seed?
If so, you are hindering your growth indeed.

She said, "You're ugly!" Have you let it go?
You are beautiful and always divine — grow!
He said, "You don't learn as fast you're an idiot, you're slow!"
You are an intelligent being, I see you reflecting the truth.
You know everything you want to know — grow!

Start nourishing your inner light and take back your power.
Affirm that you are patient with yourself every minute and every hour.
If they tell you that you're too skinny or too fat,
I would tell them I take 100% responsibility.
I accept myself in this moment right now, right where I'm at.

I can move towards all my goals with ease
because of this unconditional fact.
If they say, "I was just trying to let you know I care."
Tell them you'd prefer a hug and not a push
because now resistance is in the air.

Your father said, "You're a sissy."
Your mother said, "You're deaf and blind."
Is their challenge slamming and locking the door on your mind?
If you're happy and you know it, clap your hands and don't stoop as low.
Because you will always be perfect as you are — grow!

Tell them you were made in the image of unlimited love,
and no one can steal your joy.
You can give it to them, but they can't keep it,
no man, no woman, no girl, no boy.

True joy you will never lack when you say,
"African, Jew, Irish, Indian... I'm proud of that!"
Pull out that toxic weed; cut them some slack,
throw it away and bounce right back.
You are a creator full of vibrant visions, mysterious and grand.
With God as your guide, your burdens feel lighter than each grain of sand.

So if they say, "You're broke!" and you get that lump in your throat.
Ask yourself, "Could I let this go? Would I let this go? When?"
You may even have to let go of your poisonous friend
and find a nurturer who mends.

You have the universe at your fingertips, and you are a shining star!
Like Earth, Wind and Fire, sing no matter who you are.
I can see you basking in your inner glory and there's a glow.
I can see you harnessing your light continue to blossom and grow!
Forget about yesterday, and it is a given tomorrow may never come.

You can claim your present.
Eat your cake.
You don't need to settle for a crumb.
I see you planting healthy seeds and reaping what you sow.
When you water your thoughts they grow!

"Believe. No pessimist ever discovered the secrets of the stars,
or sailed to an uncharted land,
or opened a new heaven to the human spirit."
—Helen Keller

Your smile is the sun

Your smile is the sun that warms me.
I bathe in the miracle of light because you beam.
Dance in your yellow fields in Summer.
Sing in your red Fall and jump into your Spring.
When winter is heavy,
you are the silver lining on cloud nine where I escape to rest.
When pain brings a stream of tears.
I focus on your rainbow above the mountain's crest.
I'll travel to distant moons when stars no longer shine.
Only to realize there's never been a stronger love.
Your love is unconditional.
Your love...
Divine.

for the blooming body

Glide

Back squared, head high
You walk with meaning and purpose
Just caught a glance as I drove by
You must have a long memory
Purple majesty is in your bones
Think I just caught a love jones!

You stride with a pride unseen for blocks
Concrete can't hold you
You have the key to every lock
Because you glide like
You own chariots of gold

A man of honor
Your spirit unfolds
Your presence is felt
You glide to every beat
Time follows the direction of your feet
Yes, you are poetry in motion
Regal
Dictating time
A smile as equally fine
I wish
      I wish
            I wish

                     you were mine

Red Wine

It's going to cost you, but you're guaranteed to feel fine
A ripe red wine
A smart selection
Never watered down, mixed up, never shaken or on the rocks
So smooth, when she goes down, your vision gets clear
She relaxes you and tunes up your ear
You continue to tip the glass and ting
You've made another wish on the brim of a crystal ring

    Ting...

For she's the reason
Three more cheers for she's vibrant
She shares your love for cozy celebrations
Did I mention she's seasoned?
       (Bites back like she's seasoned.)
Changing rhythm and rhyme
A slow wine causing you to unwind like the faithful
If she were in my hand, I'd be giddy and grateful
Because she's bold
The fullness of her flavor flatters your very soul
You begin to fear if you're truly in her class
Damn the stem...It's half past the time to be prim
Hold her at the bottom of her glass
If she swirls... she 'll release a bouquet
As her aroma rises take the final sip with no delay
You want her stain to marry your dry lips
Are you dreading the end of the trip?
You instantly long for the aftertaste
She has an effect on you
I see it in your face
Don't worry a drop will linger on your tongue
Let go
You and your concoction are one
You must realize you were connected from the start
Yes, a *little* red wine is good for your heart

Swing Low

Told him I could sing.
He said,

> "That don't mean a thing.
> Performance is key.
> Don't bore me!"

Yes I can sing but it don't mean a thing. (Do Wop)
Swing batter, batter, swing... another hit!
It's all about popping that thing.
It's all about bling blang bling.
Do you have an image that goes cha-ching?
It's not where's the beef?
It's where's the buns?
When talent don't mean a thing.
He said talent don't mean a thing. (Do Wop)

The words swung out of his mouth and landed in *my* head.
I lost all of my energy and felt like I was dead.
It's that swing I dread.

Swing low, sweet chariot
Coming for to carry me home

I'm coming for your listening pleasure.
It's truly my pleasure you see.
Swinging makes you go, "Oohwee!"
How refreshing!
Get it while it's hot!
She gives that rhythm everything she's got.
Ella, how do you swing like you do?
Making the whole world see some dignity in you.
Making the whole world sing, *Zippidee do da zippidee ay!*
I shine like a daughter of light so I'm similar to a Ray.
Except I've been exposed to the mad and the gay.
In the Lord's house I'll stop and look around...
if I get there before you do.

Coming for to carry me home
I'll cut a whole and pull you through
Coming for to carry me home

My home goes with me.
Where my heart is my spirit will be.
This vessel is only your mere image of me.
I mean everything is everything.
It's all about what's seen on your TV screen.

So swing low... don't forget to zippidee do doe.

Yo!
Wait!
I've been hit!
Stop the violence, who threw that blow?
Who swung at me?

You don't like that image?
I'm sorry I was just...
I was just being me.

Yo, Yo, Yo, I'll change my flow.

Cash moves everything around me.
Where's the indoe? What?
I can smoke you like indoe...

G.

Wait... do I really have to swing that low?

Have you ever laughed?

Have you ever laughed so hard it hurt the side of your lungs?
So hard, joy and pain became one?
You couldn't stop and didn't care.
You couldn't stay put in your chair.
Have you ever lost your cool and resembled a kid in preschool?
Just like a happy hyena you caught the giggles and started to shake with glee.
Shucking and jiving like you're no more than the tender age of three.
Were you told the proper lady doesn't laugh?
She smiles, sighs politely and just grins.
But heaven knows, when I'm tickled, I can't pretend.
Laughter is my only goal and eventually I begin to rock and roll.
My face turns pink when chuckling upright
and then my body goes into shock.
It is not a pretty sight.
My laughter makes me look goofy. I try to cover my mouth.
That's when it escapes and takes a much-needed trip down south.
You might as well call me "Queen Dufus Dufey" and it's over then.
I start to embarrass people and laughter becomes my best and *only* friend.
Begin to slide around on the floor because my knees get weak.
Laugh until my arms, legs, and belly get sore and my eyes weep.
I'm rolling around, going into that knee slapping, hysterical,
I do mean berserk kind of fit?
The joke is on me and I try to fight it but it won't quit.
Somehow the joke gets glued to my funny bone...
That's where every sense of humor likes to roam.
Now when others laugh at your laughter; they might point and scream,
"Hey, look!"
Especially if your laugh sounds like a crook: "hmmn mmmhn mmhm"
like an owl: "whoooh who who"
or a hissing snake: "sss sss sss"
And if your laugh just simply sounds fake: "Ahar har har, Oh Boy, Ahar har"
You know, laughter is like fingerprints and each one is truly unique.
If you've never laughed, I mean really laughed,
one day you're in for a treat.
Don't forget to listen for the sound of laughter up and down the street.
Remember your laughter is the language your soul speaks.

> *"You grow up the day you have the first real laugh at yourself."*
> — *Ethel Barrymore*

Come Correct (for chickens and sitting ducks)

My heart races in the night
It's not fright. It's pain.
I'm searching for unspoken words.
I'm searching for a regal name.
The pressure is on me to be
a sexpot, some broken egg, sizzling hot!
I will not seduce!
I will not produce! I am not produce!
I will not be served on your breakfast tray.
And as for a roll in the hay,
Not today!
I'm not what you call a bitter chick in the street.
Street walker, Street talker
working nine-to-five ain't even me.
If I choose to live in the open like a chicken
I'm only clucking when I feel free.
I'm only clucking when I can frolic on land and still think clearly.
The tunnel to love isn't between the legs of the hen or the duck.
I am the soaring eagle that refuses to be gobbled up.
I refuse to be drafted like your first round pick.
Half the time your love feels like a long thick brick
presssssssssssssssing over me.
I could live forever free of this strain.
You say I'm insane or it's chemicals in my little birdbrain.
Because... everybody's gotta have it, right?
You say just spread eagle then one last time.
Cluck You!
It's always on your meaty mind.
If you could read my thoughts,
you'd find sensual visions and dusty talk flowing freely sometime.
Yet, I want someone to speak to me three dimensionally.
Bring me what is natural, fresh, and rare!
I need physical, spiritual, and emotional love.
It is my water, food, and air
For the flowers that grow in my green mind
On the sunny side, I'm far from over easy
On the sunny side, I'm far from over easy
On the sunny side, I'm far from over easy
If you want to tap the tantalizing tail feather on this spine,
better start unscrambling what is divine
and giving up some quality time!
I said, I want some clucking quality time.

44

Flying Fanatic Free (for body guards)

A luminary's programming crowds the brain
Question: Should privacy be traded for fame?
Read, love, and heed the message
Let the captive who captivates free
A shooting star took the fall
In search of passions that are viewed publicly
Not coming from a ghetto hood
But dumb-dumb misunderstood girl was I

Before...

    She led us through the abyss and we erased the lie

    Today don't have time to explore a third eye
    The cyclops is missing more than a parasitic truth
    Let us trade valuable signatures my child
    Let us call it a truce
    Found treasure in my empty caboose
    Had to burn the twisted noose
    Pain passes through this station
    One hundred percent proof
    The phoenix will rise whether or not you choose to see
    Your chosen name is your destiny
    You'll dance with the wind

    Setting the prophet free
    You'll arise at dawn
    Without forming a pattern of V
    You'll arise at dawn
    With no need for prophecy

The moons and suns of light, Eve, Isis, and Mary all have a common plight
To keep the Supreme Mother on the left and the Holy Father on the right
When making a wish on higher heights
daughters and sons of God, prepare for solo flight

*"Our deepest fear is not that we are inadequate. Our deepest fear is
that we are powerful beyond measure." — Marianne Williamson*

The Hot Seat

Walked into the shadow
To escape the heat of humility
She was pasted with perspiration
He never knew her dreams
Never saw her twirl or tango in the breeze
Lost sight of her position
Her under arms dripped slow like streaming faucets
The myth, she's confident and dry
As she sat on the grill with no cushion
Longing for a short skirt
In a daydream she performed a sleeveless routine
Meanwhile he removed his red tie and beckoned the waiter
He even unbuttoned his white collar as she gave a modest smile
With one nod he granted her a choice of words
She said,

     "I'll have what he's having."
He said,

     "You know I like you. You're really cool!"

That's how he became her fan

Torture

You torture me when you sit in that hard chair
Twisting and stroking your hair
I want to be the strand that just sits there
Between your fingers for fun
Want you to feel me throb until we beat as one
We can lose sight of the world's fast pace
I want you to sit on a bed of soft satin and lace

You torture me when you sit in that hard chair
Stretching your arms and spreading your chest
Arching your back like a male bird in season,
Pretending I'm not the reason you create curves like that
I'd prefer to be the reason you never hold back
In full control, submission, relief or praise
I can make you feel dizzy and dazed

When you fall asleep with one leg bent
I declare
I want to be the reason you put it there
Captured and weakened by your begging eyes
Who sent you to spark my demise?
You torture me
Dream of compromise, or should I say surrender
My mind is in a heavy blender and I can end up a smoothie or a shake
Don't know how much more of this I can take

You torture me when you pull me in with your hand
In my world you are like a fly fish on land, just jump
You have the power to demand any action you choose
Like a crying wolf when you taunt to tease you lose
There's a change in tone
Especially when I know you want to induce my deepest and darkest moan
You're like a root-bound flower
Catching to the eye but mentally you're not full-grown

A wild seed doesn't wait to be pruned or plucked
My roots are covered with fertile darkness, daily new life erupts
My roots are covered in dirt but a sunflower reaches for her cup
I want you to feel free to tumble and roam
True beauty turns scum into suds and foam
That's why you don't need the heat from this flame
You need cold April showers, space, and time

47

Later if we feel the same
We'll truly blossom, detangle and unwind
From the knots and norms

Maybe you can even nibble on my neck
Explore my physical form
If you love me
You must stop the torment

Look inside yourself
Do pry
If not, you are sure to die,
having lived a twisted, self-inflicted, root-bound lie

The only question that haunts the tortured is

    "Why?"

Heavy

Heavy on my heart...
His weight is heavy on my heart.
I lay still.
Should I awaken from the dream or is this real?
The body is heavy on my heart.
If I remove one leg, will he grab mine?
If I remove one arm,
will I struggle for the right to bear my own without any harm?
The gun is in my sight.
Should I run?
Can I escape?
Free is where I want to be.
His eyes are shut, yet they rule me.
Should I take what is personal or simply flee?
Should I leave behind pieces for those who will find answers?
Who will piece together this one sided story?
A tragedy ends in a blaze of glory.
While grabbing the tote bag on the knob, the door shuts.
I hold my breath,
adjust the bag, and the hinge creaks.
I leave the strap hanging in between the crack and
what was clean is now not so neat.
I am at a new station; a room with a dismal glow.
I hear spirits speaking below.
I am here.
They must not know.
My steps are light.
Now where do I go?
Who should I fear?

I awake to a pulsing sound heavy on the ear.

I am still here.

He can hear me

My alarm and my heart kept the same time
But my tardiness was not the biggest crime
I woke up to the dreaded call

         "He was in the hall."
     "Where, at school?"
          "He got shot down!"
    "Where?"
          "Didn't you see the front page or hear? His home."
    "Oh my dear."

But he doesn't mess around, barely 5 feet tall
He lay surrounded by yellow tape in a pool of blood upstairs in the hall
In their brand new home in the hall
His crime was protecting his mother from a fatal love affair
I dropped the phone and fell to the floor
There was no one there to care

That cuckoo male "friend" happened to pull the trigger on himself, too
At fourteen I was in total disbelief that this could happen to anyone I knew
The bark of my youth fell off on a manic Monday
God took his child Ricky at a sweet and sour 16 away

I walked in slow motion through the misery and moans
of children at his wake
His mother was the dove of peace in front of a dark blue lake
What I took from his coffin is what I want you to take from me
If I die tomorrow I want you to be everything I didn't have time to be

Take a moment
To reach in the grave and grab every unfulfilled dream you see
Like moss his gifts of words grew on me
He could make you laugh if no one else could
On him I would confide because he understood
One of the friendliest boys in the neighborhood
He was the essence of cool
I use his early departure as a tool
Never would he dismiss a pretty sight so I observe day and night
His life purpose was fulfilled when he fell like a branch from our tree
He risked life and limb because for him love meant family

Movement

Closed doors fly open at the sound of gunshots across the street.
I know wherever there's smoke, there's fire.
Should the lucid migrate towards the same retreat?
Like dominoes we are touched with one sound.
One woman shot all spectators dip down, to the ground
in clear discreet movement.

That's what I'm talking about, movement.
Isn't that what the cops feel the need to control?
Some say arresting development is their goal?
They drive by in their cruisers on the beat.
They drive by in their cruisers on patrol.

He said,

"A revolution — like a revolver — is a circle, a united front that lives on a
semi-automatic block. Real revolutions create evolution so connect the dot."

The beat goes on.
"I thought I told you that we won't stop...
I thought I told you that we won't stop."
You can revolve or you can rise like water in a foam-filled pot.
Movements are not married to an unlawful or bloody crime.

She said,

"One false move, and your king and queen is mine."

So I suggest you add new ingredients or flavors of the seasoned kind.
When you just turn up the heat and react, it's only a matter of time.
Bubbles will begin to pop. Water will begin to break.
Movement is a force that takes, with very little warning.
We awake to a high caliber of movement, each and every morning.

"All change is not growth; all movement is not forward." —
Ellen Glasglow

Stand

It's not always easy to stand up for what is right
Sometimes you'll want to turn off your inner light

First search for the good in each and every situation
But if your heart and feet feel light obey the sensation

There is also a time to run, dance, climb, and fly
But have you learned to stand and face love and the lie
But if you constantly look around for someone else's cue
The artist may leave the stage without a gift from you

After you've truly listened to a woman or man
Don't be afraid to show them where you stand
Stand in the joy, the sorrow, fear, and pain
Stand when they point, tease, and place blame

Stand in the midst of the fire on dry land
Stand because you have faith in Mother Nature's plan
Stand as if you have a debt and your life is the toll
Stand for everything and everyone who supports your goal

Step

Single
Tiny
Expression of
Power

One day and one thing at a time
A single tiny step with my left
My right wants to fall in line
I move towards every goal
Every goal that satisfies my soul
I am closer to my highest vision
I welcome the darkness of decision
I am expressing my light and power
Minute by minute
I am that patient, blossoming flower
I am open and no longer resist
Come sun
Come rain
I persist

"I figured if I said it enough, I would convince the world that I really was the greatest." — Muhammad Ali

Dance with Me

I want to dance with somebody.
I *love* to dance sometimes it puts me in a trance.
When I dance it's not like anything I know.
Don't matter if the music is fast or slow.
Don't mean to put on a show.
Just like to dance.
My heart keeps this beat.
It's super sweet.
My soul searches for what it seeks.
Can't explain it.
Wish I could tame it.
Ya'll need to follow me through history.
It all started with that drum, you see.
First I started to hum.
Then I began to pat my tum to that drum.
Then came the side step.
It was a feeling I'll never forget, made me fret.
I was like, "What's coming over me?"
Couldn't stand still.
Got a thrill from that song.
Knew I wouldn't be side stepping long.
Had to clap my hands and stomp my feet.
I was moving you see... Holy Spirit got to me.
So I did a spin around, did a dip; then I got down, pound for pound.
I had a story to tell so I picked up my friend.
We danced ourselves from heaven to hell.
Oh it wasn't always me, it was my spirit talking see.
She said "Dance... Dance with me!"
"I want to dance with somebody
Some body who loves me!"
So we danced my spirit and me
We're still dancing. See?
My mind, my body, and I got a soul that flies free.
Every time she says, "Dance... Dance with me!"
It's the dance of my spirit and me
Mind, body, and spirit are free
It's the dance of trinity
I'm dancing the trinity
"Dance!"
Come on and dance with me?

I run

I was born to run. The first time I kicked in the womb
my race had begun. And I am running a temperature,
that will leave a blazing trail beneath my feet. Even if
the rivers in my eyes turn cold, I have a promise to keep.
I was told to, "Run!"
So I don't crawl. I run. I don't walk. I run.
I've come too far from where I started from.
It's time for me to run! The rays from the sun direct me
to the harbor, where I find energy for each one.

Who suffers from the heat exhaust? From all of the pain in the purse.
In the pocket. In the hearse. In the lock and the key.
Sometimes I trip over the hurdle. Sometimes the hurdle is me!

And when you chant and cheer. I focus on the lighthearted.
The beautiful and the divine and I smile.
Because I can see you standing by.
I can see you coaching and counting seconds in the palm of your hand.
As your thumb goes up and down, you will continue to *stand*!
And I will run across country and you will track my steps!
I will lean into the wind and pace myself because it's a long stretch.
And I'm thirsty for my last 100 meters .

So I'll drink the air that I breathe and listen for your desire
with my eyes closed I'll tighten my grip on this steel baton and
dream of igniting your torch.
I said, I daydream of being the fire that rockets you to the moon!
I'll give you freedom in your left hand and you'll pass it on.
To the next man or the next woman who can!

See the gates of heaven open.
Hear the voice loud and clear, "Well done."
I need you to help me.
I need you to help me.
I need you to help me!

Maintain the pathway.
For every lost daughter.
For every lost son.
Pick up this message.
Please deliver this message   and
Run!   Run!   Run!

for the blossoming spirit

Fly

You are protected from the moon and the sun
When flying by night, you see no one
You glide on a cool breeze through the clouds above trees
When there is a change in weather
The air is your friend and the wind is your guide
You are true beauty — soar with pride
They want to capture your spirit
Heed these words, fear it
Look to the hills for strength and move
Flee
Break into motion
Spread your wings and travel
You're free
Rotate in the storm
Seek shelter amongst the fleet when it's too warm
Rest in between flights or lag like those without direction
There are sights unseen, beyond the green mountains and blue stream
Beyond the sky
You must want to live and not die
So fly towards the horizon
Fly away
Fly from fear, corruption, destruction, and decay
You with the faith of a bumblebee
He who denies gravity
Let no earthly ground hold thee
Fly
     Fly
          Fly
               Spread your wings and fly
Create your *own* destiny, fly into infinity
But right now you must evolve with me
In darkness you choose to see
This cocoon comforts thee but tomorrow you're going to fly
Free

> "He who would learn to fly one day must first learn to stand and walk and run and climb and dance, one cannot fly into flying." — Friedrich Nietzche

Cloudy

Appearing dense at first sight
Like thick cotton pillows
Each style simply delights
Every shape, size, and type
Big and small
When alone or together
All become transparent
All

"Weather is a great bluffer. I guess the same is true of our human society — things can look dark, then a break shows in the clouds, and all is changed." — E.B. White

A Broad (for a female artist)

I'm a female   a broad
                            Extending far and wide
Floating on the wings of my ego
Stroking the air with my pride
Never holding back
        Stroking with a stride
             Stroking the cellular air
                Stroking the air with pride
      With my little broad shoulders
          and my big broad brush
              I'll fly through the air
I'm so full I swear
I swear I may overflow with rhythm

pour   out   rhyme
Every stroke broad
               Every stroke mine
I will paint the atmosphere
A stroke of genius,   you'll find
A picture divine
      It will take patience
         It will take pressure
              It will take time

Broad stroking
Stroke by stroke
         Line by line
I'm a broad
     gliding over the canvass
             in your mind

Venus to Earth

I am a meteor frozen in the midnight sky
Been different for so long
Mapped out my own direction
Rejecting the sun
Set my own fiery tone
Don't follow a Milky Way
I set a future trend
Still she's my soular sister and mirror twin
Mother Earth
She is the true Star Goddess of day and night
In the morning and evening she harbors more
Much more than light
So I keep her in my sight

Rain

As others seek cover
Let me explain I'm a lover
I marvel at the sound of water on my window
Marvel at the sound of water on my pane

It comforts me as sunshine does the sane

I'll step outside and welcome each falling drop
Hoping to be the anchor for the stop
With cupped hands and an open mouth
As a Spring breeze blows floating tears from the south

In hopes I'll beat out the walls of nearby homes for I love the taste
Love the taste of God's falling grace
Want first taste as s/he cleanses the world and rejuvenates the race
Aaaaah, a light misty melody falls slowly in the near distance

The picnic table in the yard is repainted with polka dot persistence
Each raindrop reaches a final destination and fate
Causing me to contemplate my state
My sundress lined shoulders desire to be the next palette

So I walk to the table where my uncle abandoned a salad
I take baby steps after the thunder rolls
Calculating the distance of lightning and the end of my stroll
As long as the lightning isn't near, I continue to count my toll

My scalp tingles at the thought of three drops
My right hand holds a record of five back or five top
My big toe wiggles with the thought of one
My eye could use a tear from above, it longs for random fun

Just then my lash was touched and so was my left ear
Rain in my heart and my soul
Your rain is welcome here

"Millions long for immortality but don't know what to do with
themselves on a rainy Sunday afternoon." — Susan Ertz

Rivers

Rivers are my mother's blood vessels
From this place it's so plain

The Earth resembles me and my inner mystery
A composite of creation, crosses my window in plain view
If I were thirsty, I'd drink from her crystal rivers
Her rivers represent the blue blood vessels
running through my veins

A channel brings my eyes to the bank
This is where the river meets this stream
Where I choose to ponder on deposits

Life flows inside my mother's body
Life flows inside my veins

Mother, May I

May I have the power to pollinate?
May I flower you to hate hate?
May I cause you to facilitate the debate that spins off Springer and Lake?
May I cause you to reflect on every song you heard
that implies that
       to be gay is absurd and claims
       "nigger" is the choice word and
       every Jew is out to get you and
       all women are hoes and bitches, too.

May I pollinate?
May I flower you to hate hate?
May I give birth to a flower child or your freedom before late?
May I fly away and pay pilgrimage to apple trees?
May I play in evergreen fields like honeybees?
May I skip through the daises and the leaves?
Mother, may I please?

Take one giant step?

The Bitter

"Beware
of the devil
the slinking devil
whispers...
whispers into
the hearts of men.
The message is
so faint it slowly
slithers in
from among
the gin.
It slithers
and slowly
slinks in
whispering
"Hate!"
Don't get bit by the
bitter snake!"
The bitter devil bites
bites into your soul.
Symptoms :
a sour stare,
grinding teeth,
raised hair,
terrible twitch, and
wrinkles above
a piercing glare.
If looks could kill
thousands would die.
Beware... beware
of the bitter snake!
Slinking devil
whispers and
his poisonous
venom
multiplies.
You'll believe
your only
remedy
is a lie!

Me and my Shadow

Adding depth and dimension to the tallest mountain
Many find a calm comfort in the shade

Hiding from the severe scorch
Because the dark is easy on a tainted eye
They hide in the blurry lines and edges
Only to make light of dismal duty
Me and my shadow shrink and expand

Only a shadow plays tricks
With a mirage he can
Creating a make believe land
Skyscrapers appear upside down
White-capped mountains bubble on turquoise water
We stick together
We shrink and expand

Me and my shadow
Me and my illusion

"Character is like a tree and reputation like its shadow. The shadow
is what we think of it; the tree is the real thing."
— Abraham Lincoln

Palm Readings

There are weather patterns on palms
that forecast your tidal waves.
Circles lie underneath broken pieces.
Imperfection is perfect
at six and nine.
Half moons set on cuticles at your fingertips.
The sky is clearly written on your face.
Distant roads seem near.
The path less traveled is open for exploration.
There are roads beyond the frontier.
We can journey beyond the constraints of mini maps.
We rotate differently but I still see us as the same.
We all search for direction.
Let me lead you to the center of your heart.
Palm prints are patterns
each a distinct yellow, red, white or brown mark.
Are you a molehill or a mountain?
Have you ever studied the skin you're in?
There is a unique texture in this rocky place.
Beneath the vast stretch of quicksand lies deep space.
Do you want to know the truth about your fate?
Your future is written in between the lines.
Pay attention to the gravity that grounds you.
I will dissect the patterns on your palms.
Just purchase another reading.

What lies beneath?

Rolling faster than water on dry land
These shells twirl, tip, and toe
In the stillness of night
Riding waves in the moon's glow

Rolling faster than water on dry land
Harboring life, the sea, and grains of sand

"Nobody knows the mysteries which lie at the bottom of the ocean."
— Yoruba proverb

I don't like boxes (for wild flowers)

I'm a bright yellow sunflower
Symbolizing youth, withering by the hour
Chosen like a pocketful of posies
Sniffed, as if I'm jasmine, oriental orchids, and viburnum
The adopted adapt to low lamplight like it's fun
Hand picked from an abandoned garden by a baby girl who loves the sun

Been cut, cut down to size; cut down to fit in these sharp corners
It's a caged bird's eye view where I stand
Life in a 4x5 terra cotta pot
There's tracings of moss, mystical metal, and polished rock
Wading in dingy water on the edge of a blue windowsill
Right next to a closed silver screen
Born to compliment two yellow roses near by
Live to blend into the arrangement and dream

Silent like a stillborn entering Earth
Dreaming of being replanted into fertile soil
Who has the fertile soil that will nourish my battered birth?

In my dreams we all have rugged roots
Slow dancing with a brilliant breeze
Today and everyday, we take some of the final sips
One of my pointy petals is falling like a strand of hair
The top of my stem is curving, it bends when I drift
Almost there, basking in beaming rays and living free
Like that mighty willow tree in a wide-open field

"For myself I hold no preferences among flowers,
so long as they are wild, free, spontaneous.
Bricks to all greenhouses!
Black thumb and cutworm to the potted plant!"
— Edward Abbey

That tree over there, that tree you see,
That tree keeps whispering knowledge to me.
It's a mover and a shaker but grounded by its
maker. That tree. I can see its roots are long. Sap sweeter
than a love song. How many lifetimes has it seen? I know the
weather must have been mean because that tree knows my name
and my rhyme but has no measure for time. Only respect to seasons
as it grows. That tree knows when to let go is when the winter wind
blows. Wait a minute, you can't see. You can't see the forest because of
the tree. Then take a step back with me because I don't want you to miss
the beauty of this big family. When we move in closer again, you'll see
there's beauty and there's a family inside that tree. Several species
finding comfort, from birds to ants, squirrels and even a pesky flea.
Without the production of roots, raindrops, and leaves I would not be.
So I listen. I listen when that tree speaks to me. That tree over
there you see, it tells me to spread
my branches
and shake
my
leaves...
inhale
this gift
of
oxygen
and breathe as I please.

*"Trees like to have kids climb on them, but trees are often much
bigger than we are, and much more forgiving." — Diane Frolov*

Redemption Poem (for Bob Marley)

If I were Jah I'd sing in the star lit sky with enchanted charm
March to a universal beat
They'd call me a rebel and you a militant because
You'd mirror my creation
Dancehall down every trench town street
I'd create. Zion
I'd destroy Babylon's philosophy
Dress you in red, gold, and green
Until the last crazy baldhead is tried
Until the last crazy baldhead is seen
I and I would serve for I'd be a child of life
I'd leave a lasting legacy and footprints on how to eliminate strife

If I were Jah you'd catch me playing soccer
In bright blue fresh morning air
I'd ask you to join me
I'd ask you to look inside yourself
You'll find answers there

I'd love away fears and dance to a freedom song
No woman no cry.
She would not cry for long because
If I were Jah I'd be giving
If I were Jah I'd be satisfied with the life I'm living
I'd satisfy my soul with the life I'm living
If you didn't' know what life was worth
I'd recruit you as one of Jah's people and
return you to the movement in heaven Earth
Until you'd see the light

My melody would cause you to skip to the right
Until the last of the wicked were surrounded by 50,000
heavily armed members of joy
Until the last of the wicked were surrounded by every righteous girl and boy
Until the racing rat comes running with thanks and praise on high
Singing
One love
One heart
Rastafari

"Emancipate yourself from mental slavery, none but ourselves can free our minds." — Bob Marley

70

Dali's Daddy Longlegs of the Evening Hope

My head is heavy as they dance to decay
My insides torn as we rest on what is left of the olive tree
Deaf to the sounds of Cupid's cry
Speechless because my tongue has been cut out and discarded
Music is melting
Stretched out my neck in the heat
Now we lay in a deep sleep
Two dried up bottles of ink lay on my milkless breast
An apolitical and unconscious artist is at rest as
A daddy longleg walks across my cheek
When will the war cease?
No one can forget the sound of peace
When will the exhaustion end?
Luck surfaces but hope is still somewhere within
the removal of a crutch
Oh Cupid mend me and
Mold me with your touch

She (for Tracy Chapman)

Mother Earth at her very core
She's moving and standing still
Her serenity moves me
Breathing in her sky and drinking her sea
As she grows heavy roots we change
Always producing an acoustic sound with a versatile range
Always shedding dead leaves and the stems that bring pain
Like a pure poet who makes folk music in good and bad times
Like orange and yellow leaves floating on invisible air
She's the harmonious guide that lives to nurture those who care
With patient eyes, as deep as the darkest blue river
A humble smile, that makes cold feet courageous and warm
Tracing life with her fingers she leads us through the sandstorm
She sings of a new beginning, we close our eyes in search of a story
She's healing chapped lips so they may kiss the ground of glory

"We must live our lives always feeling, always thinking the moment has arrived." — Tracy Chapman

Down, Out and Away

Take me down where the river meets the stream
Take me out in the ocean where dolphins sing
Take me away from the office fiends

Take me down in the forest we can skip through the maze
Take me out to the evergreen valley where the animals graze
Take me away from the smog and the haze

Take me down to the meadow where the reflection is clear
Take me out amongst the corn, wheat, and deer
Take me away to mountains I have nothing to fear

Take me down, out, and away

How does it feel to be an animal...a savage beast?
Who stabbed Mother Earth and still seeks to heal her by doing the very least?

How does it feel to be an animal...a beast?
Who enslaves his own and marks territory in the West and East?

How does it feel to be a beast with a basic instinct to kill?
Who hunts, murders, and cages creatures for a pet project thrill?

How does it feel to be a tamed...beast?
Who's educated but still hungers for animal flesh as a chosen feast?

> *"Until we have the courage to recognize cruelty for what it is —*
> *whether its victim is human or animal — we cannot expect things to*
> *be much better in this world...We cannot have peace among men*
> *whose hearts delight in killing any living creature. By every act*
> *that glorifies or even tolerates such moronic delight in killing, we*
> *set back the progress of humanity." – Rachel Carson*

Woodlands

In the countryside
I left memories
Remember those rolling hills
Every day we went on a coaster ride
I'd often climb in the tree to hide
Sometimes trees were evergreen
Sometimes they were covered with white crunchy blankets of snow
Rows of brown wheat would sway up ahead
Peachy sunsets would set behind our pickup, rusty Roscoe
Roads glistening with fresh flakes
Left over leaves from the autumn mixed in
Can't wait to see the red, orange, green, and yellow leaves again
If it was Spring we could pick blue berries though
Summer nights we played in the glow
The moon's always bright
Out in the bush, there's not a lot of light
Crickets brought the morning in
Could race around the block with a funny friend
Not much traffic you see
Just distant sounds of route thirty
As semi-trucks flew by
On foggy mornings the dew would blend into my eye
Walked to the bus stop as a robin took to branches that traced my way
Only one home had a chicken coop,
so it seemed to stand out at the end due to hay
Living in the woods, a land far away from the city
Meant being in the boondocks and the center of pity
In the boonies, down in the rough, they would say
But I sure do miss home today

"I grew up in this town, my poetry was born between the hill and the river, it took its voice from the rain, and like the timber, it steeped itself in the forests." — Pablo Neruda

Drink Meters

I will write in metaphor
though clearly absurd
capture music, blue harmony, surreal
appear icon
yet free the spoonless
no demand could haunt
my hand but the grave
almost has
here
a pad lives
screaming
travel
by ink
escape with a hunger
drink meters
search and seek
God is song
let rhythm speak

Dixie Land

I've been weary
Was black misery
Full of red passion but blue, walking blue
Well I heard this sound and it's true

The horn had a strange toot
Sent sensations to the base of my roots
That's a cool flute
It had cats dressed in a zoot suit doing the jitterbug while waiting in line

Stopped and asked for directions to the space and place
where I could spend my dime
No longer on the outside looking in
No stranger, I'm what you call friend

With my ten dollars in hand she says, "Thanks for coming!"
"Welcome to Dixie Land!"

The bridge begins
Packed in at 9:05
All night... live!

He flips his suspenders anticipating the play
I could watch him do that solo grind every day

He made that bell speak
She hollered, "Talk to me! Preach!"
Then he'd do this hip walk

That made all the girls weak
Bass had braids and trumpet had a fro

The sax man was bright, he phoned with a glow
He blew my mind cool as silver riffs rippled on the cymbal
Ahhhhh... the chimes

But there was nothing like a shot of rim from my Buddy Rich
He turned into the boom clack at the end of every line

Boom-clack, like that
He'd did it again
That's when....

The Piano man began to tip toe fingers along my heart
A midnight blues set starts

His voice floated through that smoky room
That soulful melody sparked a flame
We could taste eternal love, I released all guilt and shame

The dark cornea of my right eye became misty
And my aching heart bled light

Colorful keys took me to a place up the scales
As he tended the torn with tales of deliverance
Caramel fingers tracing ivory milk and I tapped

Tapped out of the hell that society built
Baby it was grand

Just then...The lead vocalist rose from his bench
Strolled to the center of the band
With a black hat in hand

He threw it in the air, spun around, and
caught it on the tip of his spit shined shoe

Boom-clack

The drum did a soft roll and
Silence took its toll, giving way
to a thunderous and gracious crowd

We hooted a constellation of praises...
Loud!

Do you know what they did?
They bowed.

Swing Jazz Cats (for Ella Fitzgerald)

The Crusaders charged in like a herd when the crowd began to stray.
They said,"We're Picking up the Pieces!"
"The average big bands left yesterday."
This time we wanted to do something more than a simple side sway.
So we made some naughty noise.
Girls started bouncing like baby boys.
'Cuz that beat was jumpin'.
I mean really jumpin'!
Flipping and twisting them girls like toys!
Me? No, I ain't misbehavin'!
But 'Out of the Blue' Daddy O had left.
"What it is, Cat?" Lady Scat taking us back. She said,

> It don't mean a thing if it ain't got that swing
> Doo Wop /Doo Wop /Doo Wop /Doo Wop /Doo Wop/Doo Wop
> It don't mean a thing, all you got to do is sing.
> Doo Wop /Doo Wop /Doo Wop /Doo Wop /Doo Wop/DooWop
> It makes no difference if it's sweet or hot
> Just give that rhythm ev'rything you got ta goo got!
> Bada da Boo Bot /Skada Do Bop/Skee dee Do Wop
> Doo Wa Ga ot Bee Da Boo ot Wa ot Doo Wa Wop

Whoa!
Ella was so full she blew up the spot.
Ooo Sha Bam, 'Bean a Re Bop' KaZam!
That joint was hot and heavy!
Grooving on a highway for Miles with Freddy.
Frankie knows it was a Maze of movement.

Thighs,
Heels,
Every toe tapping and I always meant to say,
 "I got a kick out of you!"

She'd just say,
"Baby, love is here to stay. You be sweet."

I guess it just means there will always be Spring in my feet.
I decided to get on up so I could get on down.
These weary blues will never ever make me lose my beat.

Poem no. 10803 (for Nikki Giovanni)

This is not a poem about Nikki Giovanni
This is a poem about a spicy spirit that's so bodacious
It bites like fresh, red hot pepper mixed in a signature sauce
Tongues become numb, that's the cost
The taste is clearly bold
So rare, it reminds you of big red diamonds or pure black gold
The spirit can be seen in the twinkle of Nikki's eyes,
comes from a seasoned soul
But this is not a poem about Nikki Giovanni
This is about a spirit that's ancient and old
It stared fear in the face and was Queen Nandi's secret mold
It's Queen Hatshesput's glue and Queen Nefertiti's piquant plan
This spirit is what makes grown men fear a scorned woman

When asked the beholder of such a savored spirit

>"How do you say it so raw making a complex blend
>taste like oysters on the half shell — juicy yet pleasantly plain?"

>She said, "It's the truth."
>The truth is a spirit that should awaken the senses and
>never be tamed. You either embrace it, or live in a bland shame!

This is not a poem about Nikki Giovanni
But remember her name and the bold taste that brought her fame

>She said, "They want us to stand for America,
>Until the America on record is black.
>They don't understand me? Hell, I don't understand that!"

You can still find her speaking her truth, as a matter of fact

She loves the bitter
She loves the sweet
She loves the heat
Of her *own*
Spice rack!

>*"It's better to take a chance and be wrong than to be safe and dull."*
>*– Nikki Giovanni*

Creativity – Kuumba (koo- OOM-bah)

Afrikans have made vast contributions since nativity!
But there have been some who sought to discredit
all who are creative and black like me.

The architecture of pyramids.
Monotheism, mathematics, astrology, and philosophy
made the hungry for knowledge drool.
When Africa educated the world,
some say, even Jesus and Buddha went to Egyptian mystery school.

Today some still follow an ancient eastern philosophy and plan.
Leave future generations with better tools and better land.
If you were never taught about black American contributions
I'll name a few.

The Red Cross is very grateful for the very first blood bank,
created by Dr. Charles Drew.
Oscar E. Brown put his lock and key on the horseshoe.
Benjamin Bannecker built America's very first clock.
He also planned and designed the nations capital from bottom to top.
Benjamin Bannecker, don't forget his name.
He created a world almanac that earned him international fame.

Now Charles B. Brooks, he developed a unique street sweep.
You couldn't iron your clothes on a decent board
until Sarah Boone wanted you to look neat.
Thomas Jennings received the first black patent for dry clean.
Brush your hair and think of Lydia Newman.
She never wanted one stubborn strand to be seen!

Representing ladies world wide, the first female self-made millionaire:
Madame C.J. Walker.
She took pride in her comb and was a smooth talker with a mind of her own.
He's credited with over 300 ideas like bleach, ink, instant coffee.
The man was an agricultural genius too.
It's George Washington Carver, the first to put peanut butter on your menu.
Stroll across your lawn and think of the mower John Burr perfected for you.

William Purvis improved the fountain pen because
John Love's pencil sharpener was no longer in.
Lee Burridge most likely said, "I can top all that you just bet...
I'll make me a typewriter so I can print the message with inkjet!"

81

One day, Frederick M. Jones was hot but he had to be really cool.
He improved the air conditioner and now AC is the rule!
We can have refrigerated drinks all because of that Jones.
He knew just how to think!
When Lonnie Johnson was hot, he also used his head.
He created the Super Soaker... it's the one water gun we dread!

Wish I could personally thank Garrett Morgan for the gas mask.
Testing that product must have been a breath-taking task!
If I'm in smoke, don't have to choke, and I can see.
With Morgan's traffic signal on the road,
there are less fools trying to run over me!
Alexander Miles invented the elevator and Harry Hopkins the hearing aide.
Henry T. Sampson invented the cell phone.
Maybe you will help prevent the signal fade.

Lewis Latimer helped Edison and Graham
provide the means for you to telephone me.
There's another invisible man, brace yourself or
get ready to say, "Whoa, Nelly"
He's Dr. Mark Dean, developed twenty patents with a Stanford degree.
A founding father of the computer, a black man gave birth to your PC.
During a biological tragedy, we also have a small pox vaccine.
It was Dr. Louis Wright, he's known as a one-man medical team.
Patricia Bath discovered that laser eye surgery technique.
She wanted you to see that clearly the future is far from bleak.

So if you're black, yellow, white, brown, or blue and
still think there's no creativity in you?
Say, "I can make the world a better place....
I create ideas and make choices that benefit the entire human race."

Kuumba is creativity; in Kwanzaa this is the sixth day
We will weigh this principle carefully and give grace

Ase (ah-shay)

*"It is creative potential itself in human beings
that is the image of God." —Mary Daly*

Ize Free (for Ize Ofrika)

Like the Fall at Summer's end,
I turned around and the kids were in school again.
It sneaks up on you.

With you, it was always quiet and quick.
You were never fond of telling lies.
Never was one for saying goodbyes.
You say we give it too much thought.
Sometimes we pause, do that uneasy laugh or change the subject.
We review and reflect like a professor preparing for thesis.
You denied me the comfort of the seal.
Open   like a letter.
Going through the postal system.
Prey for the curious.

Should I just let it go?
Where did you go?
How do I know?

I stood open to misinterpretations.
A transmission interrupted, a grey signal fade,
Static   wanting to cling.

Why didn't you stay in this station?
I was in the channel without a paddle, and you taught me vibration.

I didn't want to be muted.
I didn't want you to use the remote.
I didn't want you to push my buttons from far away.

But you often denied me this one simple word.
After all, those who live longer than butterflies,
grow accustomed to the emptiness it brings.

My grandmother, with her lead foot, rides the road so much better.
She's a racing rat trapped in a wrinkled elephant's body.
I too am an elephant and those past lives I remember.
How could I forget? No saint is ever in a hurry.
But boy did you leave in a scurry. I know.
You were never fond of telling lies.
Never was one for saying good byes.

Like the Fall at Summer's end,
I turned around and the kids were in school again.
Like those who played hooky you escaped.
Like an enslaved African, you were flying.
You were fueled with hope unaware of the eternal fate.
In the spirit of Tubman, you trailed in a blaze
through this underground word road.
In pitch-black night, you chose the journey of a blind man.
You'd prefer to have your eyes scratched out
than to stare at the sight of dependence.
It was the blind leading the "color blind" again.
Yes, I could see cascading colors to no end.

The only thing you wanted me to see, was me
standing up, standing tall and, if need be, alone.
Here I am sinking into the sands of time.
I am asking for a final hug or a kiss.
Well okay, I agree too many can take a toll.
The way it parts your lips with a quick roll.
"Bye"
and silence echoes,
silence follows,
I was just singing.

"Bye and bye, when the morning comes all God's children will come together
as one. Tell the story how we overcome and we'll understand it better bye
and bye."

But until then,
you'd rather me say, "Go!"
You'd rather stand up and go.

"Go ye therefore and teach all nations,
Go!
Go!
Go!"

Do you see a three-letter word on the palm of my hand?
B-Y-E bring your eyes!
Those big, deep, dark eyes black man.
I want you to see the children of the sun rising.
God and Goddess will return on land and this time I want you to see.
Eyes free of pain and I even let go of fear my friend.
I just want you to see.
Ize Free.

Poetic Soldier (for Pablo Neruda)

A poetic soldier waits in line for the word   *"Forward!"*
Pablo speaks of passion in his formal address
He speaks of the sweet waste of America and his detest of
Chile's chaotic civil war and the constant state of unrest
A poetic soldier is in step leading with his *left*
Searching for a way to stoically step out of line
But his truth still marches on and
The voice of the people never *left* his mind
He's *left* with an after taste
You can see a pinch of love *left* in his hard face
So they stampede his home in a whirlwind of ripened rage
Seeking to burn and tear each word *left* from the page
Some Nobel Peaceful march this is

                                    "Ready... Halt!"

Love is what it is
The calming stream that warms us with rippling waves
Drenching dry feet and healing cracked hands
Giving hope to every woman and every man
May this stream flow to distant shores
May it quench the center of the earth's core
From every dying house
From every dying cell and pore
You may find me in exile with the next oust
When democracy doesn't live here any more
You may find me in exile because I purify the open sore
When freedom doesn't live here any more
A poetic soldier prized with a red heart waits
As clones seek to puncture, ransack, and kill
The spirit lives on, as they drill the mind
In an effort to keep the flock bleeding in battle
In an effort to keep the flock blind
An ambassador to their clear conscience
With belted, brass books that shine
We are the people's passion
A poetic soldier is a dictator's deadliest assassin

Even in death Pablo you are more than a metaphor or a rhythmic line
You keep giving hope to the homeless
You keep giving sight to the blind

                                    "Forward... March!"

85

Perfect Time

You *are* progressing and your path is clear
If your purpose was fulfilled you would no longer be here
You *are* in the right place and everything is just fine
When we stay open to the possibilities
The process is the reason and rhyme

Everything happens in perfect time
Everything happens in perfect time

When we start to rush we lose our minds
No need to speed up
No need to rewind
Have faith and take your time
Enjoy the rising and the setting of the sun
Enjoy the journey of one
Your blessings will fall in line

Everything happens in perfect time

When in the moment you're destined to shine
Just surrender and take back your peace of mind
Just surrender *all* and take back your peace of mind

> *"Brothers and sisters, take your time.*
> *If only we could see we must be kind.*
> *Knowledge and wisdom we will find.*
> *All things happen in perfect time."*

The seasons are unfolding
If we run too fast, the trees become blurry and we become blind
To the beauty of the Creator's will and design
Unplanned events add suspense
Develop your courage and confidence
When we walk in with intuition
When we open up our hearts and make up our minds
Worry and frantic fear erupts
So we slow down and fill our spiritual cups
When we're full of grace and faith we can dream, build, or climb
When we stay open to the possibilities
The process is the reason and rhyme

Everything happens in perfect time

Amen (for female teachers and preachers)

Let me hear you say "Amen!"
Somebody say it again
See a man destroyed my home when he left a woman alone
A man made me groan then he changed his tone
A man ripped off my shirt and groped me in a crowd
A man yelled, "Look at her stupid ass!" and laughed real loud
He didn't see me as his sister, a friend, or as a mother
Oh, no. I was simply the foe, a female, a woman, a hoe.
A man made me feel like I couldn't say, "No!"

Misogynist is the title of these artists who find instant fame
Simply by calling a female outside her name
But this type of music is not banned in your store
Why? Mama bought it for A man
Somebody say, "Amen!"
And the CD case is on her daughter's bedroom floor
Because as long as a woman sees herself as less than
A man doesn't have to be more
Somebody said we need a woman of state
Somebody say, "Awomen!"
Wait a minute...

I Timothy chapter 2 verses 11-14 is cause for debate.
Quiet as it's kept, King James was openly bisexual.
He never knew his mother and he passed on more
chauvinistic than homophobic traits.
"Kings are rightly called Gods," he'd say
and if you don't believe my version, it's hell you'll pay.

Well today, if you really want to see equal economic opportunity
sister, clean up your inner temple, and help organize your community.

And can I get my brother to cherish a parental role
that's not based on your gender fate?
Could you imagine every single man knowing how to fix his own plate?

And if your son has a sense of male pride,
I say let him play with the doll and nurture the father inside.
Maybe your daughter can learn how to protect herself,
just in case, someone decides to run and hide?

That's when the violence will decrease.
Can we strive for the 22nd century at least?

Because your son's war games and toy soldiers are *played out*
in the west, north, east, and south.
Can I get a woman to stop raising these extreme men?
I don't want to hear of these types of men again.

For it is a woman that we've all passed through,
therefore, to every woman, respect is due.

So when we say "Amen," can we all say "Awomen," too?
And may this new sense of balance be the much-needed glue?

Okay. Let us pray.

Dear Creator Mother and Father God of the heavens and the earth,
May each and every one of your creations feel a sense of worth?
May harmony and balance return to our visions again?
Let it be so.
And so it is.

Awomen. Amen.

*"Misogynist: A man who hates women as much as women hate one
another."* — H. L. Mencken

She Rose

She didn't go to the market that day.
She put all material cares away.
In spite of feeling torn and beat, she rose.

From dirt roads and paved concrete, she rose.
Stood front and center in that raging rally.
With a heavy heart, she smiled in the valley.

She said, "Wake up! This is the *last* time.
I need you to put your hand in mine."

Her voice rings loud in my ear.

She rose   to strengthen the family.
She rose   and faced her fear.